GOD
Behind the Scenes

JOSEPH'S LIFE STORY

Dr. Aaron R. Jones

GOD BEHIND THE SCENES: JOSEPH'S LIFE STORY

Copyright © 2019 by Dr. Aaron R. Jones

Printed in the
United States of America

Published by Kingdom Publishing, LLC
Odenton, Maryland

All rights reserved. No part of this book may be reproduced or transmitted in any form or by any means, electronic or mechanical, including photocopying, recording or by any information storage and retrieval system without written permission from the author, except for the inclusion of brief quotations in a review.

All scripture quotations are from the King James Version of the Bible. Thomas Nelson Publishers, Nashville: Thomas Nelson, Inc. 1972, Public Domain. Scripture quotations noted NIV are from the Holy Bible: New International Version® Copyright © 1973, 1978, 1984 by International Bible Society. Used by permission of Zondervan Publishing House. All rights reserved.

Editor: Sharon D. Jones
Copyeditor: Kimberly Curtis
Artist: Pastor Reggie Pickett
Dr. Aaron R. Jones
ISBN: 978-0-9961267-2-4
Library of Congress Control Number: 2019911298

TABLE OF CONTENTS

Foreword   5

Introduction   7

4 Principles for Behind the Scenes
- Principle #1 - God is moving, even when we don't see it.   12
- Principle #2 - God is unique.   15
- Principle #3 - What is sudden to man is not sudden to God.   18
- Principle #4 - Just because it looks like there is no hope; it doesn't mean God is not near.   20

Scene #1 Joseph Finds Favor   23

Scene #2 God Shows Joseph a Dream   29

Scene #3 Satan is Always Active   35

Scene #4 The Anointing Recognized   41

Scene #5 Compromise is Not an Option   47

Scene #6 Grace with Potiphar   53

Scene #7 Favor in Prison   57

Scene #8 Your Gift Will Make Room For You   63

Scene #9 The Dream Comes to Pass   69

Scene #10 God Will Turn It Around   75

Epilogue Joseph and Jesus   81

FOREWORD

Everyone who God created has the potential of fulfilling God's will for their lives. This potential is actuated when we choose to live a life in intimate relationship with God. You will find out that the world is a big stage where your life is dramatized; the people you meet and the situations you go through are the scenes of your life that will ultimately culminate into a great story.

However, we don't know the story that's been set for us, neither the script that's been written. The only way to find out how to play your part of being YOU is to communicate with the director of the story.

"God Behind the Scenes," Dr. Aaron Jones masterfully and gracefully shares with us how God was heavily involved in Joseph's eventful life, through every difficult situation until the time he was set up to be second in command in all of Egypt.

Like Joseph, sometimes we don't know why we experience certain hardships and what is to become of us afterwards, but we must trust that someone is working behind the scenes to make sure that it'll all work out for our good - that someone is God Himself. There are certain principles that we all can learn from how God dealt with Joseph that we, too, can apply to our lives and fulfill God's will and see our great story unfold.

Bishop Antonio M. Palmer
Kingdom Celebration Center
Odenton, Maryland

INTRODUCTION

Life's trials and tribulations seem to grow daily and can seem insurmountable. As believers, we may not understand why we experience specific challenges or how we will live through the challenges, but we must have faith and believe in God's word. We realize life was never promised to be easy. However, we were promised peace through Christ Jesus. John 16:33 tells us, *"These things I have spoken unto you, that in me ye might have peace. In the world, ye shall have tribulation: but be of good cheer; I have overcome the world."*

If you know that God has called you to a greater future, but you feel stuck in a mediocre or discouraging present, continue to be faithful. God working behind the scenes during our challenges encourages the believer that hope is always near.

What is meant by the phrase, *"Behind the Scenes?"* The definition of behind the scenes is revelation of things that normally happens privately or without someone's knowledge. "Behind the scenes" are happenings that are known to some, but unknown to others.

In every area of our lives, which we cannot see, God is working out His will. God sees all and knows all. Hebrews 4:13 says, *"Nothing in all creation is hidden from God's sight. Everything is uncovered and laid bare before the eyes of him to whom we must give account."*

God wants us to trust Him, when it seems like He is not present. God is constantly moving on our behalf, so that all things will work together. When we least expect it, God is preparing or repairing something in our lives. No matter what you are going through, God is working it out for your good. Romans 8:28 says, *"And we know that all things work together for good to them that love God, to them who are called according to his purpose."* The Apostle Paul causes the believer to look beyond what may be going on in the physical because God always has a divine plan. Therefore, our good and bad days will result in good.

Although the barriers along life's journey may be uncertain, keep moving forward and holding on to the faith that you know to be true. Trust God, even when you don't understand. In these times, you cannot begin to doubt God and trust your ideas, but continue to keep all things in His hands. At all times, God wants to be the pilot. Proverbs 3:5, 6 gives a life plan: *"Trust in the LORD with all thine heart; and lean not unto thine own understanding. In all thy ways acknowledge him, and he shall direct thy paths."*

In any significant assignment, program, production, event, or project, there are always actions taking place behind the scenes.

As believers, we rest in the fact that God is working behind the scenes on our behalf. We need to take comfort in knowing there is always more for us than against us. You may be going through the struggle of your life, trust and know God is there in the dark moments. Even when we make bad decisions or try to run from God, He is there. I love what the psalm writer says in Psalm 139:8, *"If I ascend up into heaven, thou art there: if I make my bed in hell, behold, thou art there."*

However, we should also recognize the closer we get to God and our dreams (the next stage or phase in our life) the more suffering, trials, and tribulations we may experience. Second Timothy 3:12 says, *"Yea, and all that will live godly in Christ Jesus shall suffer persecution."* When we know

God is working on our behalf, it helps us to hold fast through our trials and tribulations.

In this book, I have included four behind the scenes principles that can be used as frames of reference when trials and tribulations present themselves in your life. The truths these principles reveal may become the foundation of our trust in God while He works behind the scenes.

BEHIND THE SCENES

Principles

Principle #1

~~~~~~~~~~~

God is moving, even when we don't see it.

~~~~~~~~~~~

As life happens, God is continuously active behind the scenes. We may not know fully or understand initially, but God is in charge. He is sovereign in all His ways. His sovereignty should bring a daily sense of peace.

As believers, we are encouraged to stay faithful to God (regardless of what it may look like in the natural). We shouldn't be so drawn by what we see, because that may be deceiving. When we focus on what we see in the physical, we take our eyes off the Lord. Now, the focus is on our situation.

Psalm 121:1, 2 encourages us to keep our eyes on the Lord: *"I will lift up mine eyes unto the hills from which cometh my help, my help cometh from the Lord."* This is the source or our strength. I want to encourage you to never make a decision based solely on what you see on the outside. The Apostle Paul says, "things that we see are temporary, but the things we don't see are eternal (2 Corinthians 4:18)." Our awesome God designs our destiny.

We must continue to move forward, even when we cannot see everything presented before us. Athough we know what we see is real, we must decide to walk by faith in the word of God. 2 Corinthians 5:7 says, *"For we walk by faith, not by sight."* This verse does not mean we ignore reality, but we know that what we see is not the end of the story. What we see should not determine what we believe God can do.

What are you seeing today? It doesn't have to be the end, because God is working something out on your behalf. This principle can also be referred to when you experience *"curtain peace."* For example, when you watch a play and the curtain closes, you know the current scene has ended. When the curtain opens, the next scene begins with updates and changes. "Curtain peace" occurs when you exercise your faith and believe that God is handling everything behind the scenes to bring about His best for the next phrase in your life. Not seeing does not mean not happening. You don't know what is going on, but things are changing.

There are times when God is silent, and you don't know what God is saying or doing. You still must believe that He is actively moving things and changing situations in your life. Your faith tells you something is working, and God is up to something.

Principle #2
~~~~~~~~~~~
God is unique.
~~~~~~~~~~~

The Bible declares, there is no God like our God. He is a God that stands alone and is holy. We should not try to calculate how or what God will do. We cannot forecast or predict how He will respond. This is why He is God. Isaiah tells us, God's thoughts are not our thoughts; neither are our ways His ways (Isaiah 55:8). God's higher ways and thoughts indicate He exceeds our knowledge and abilities.

The birth and life of Jesus declare the uniqueness of God. As believers, we expect the Savior to be kingly, born from royalty with the best of the best. We often reject things that do not fit within the realm of our expectations. 1 Peter 2:4 says, *"To whom coming, as unto a living stone, disallowed indeed of men, but chosen of God, and precious."* We see humility through the birth of Jesus. He is the King of Kings and Lord of Lord, yet he was born in a manger (a place fit for animals). His earthly father's trade was that of a carpenter (builder)—a job, taking orders from someone else. Can you imagine our Lord cutting, shaping, and building your house?

Jesus was a carpenter, but was known as the cornerstone, the ROCK that built the church. 1 Peter 2:6, 7—*"Wherefore also it is contained in the scripture, Behold, I lay in Sion a chief corner stone, elect, precious: and he that believeth on him shall not be confounded. Unto you therefore which believe he is precious: but unto them which be disobedient, the stone which the builders disallowed, the same is made the head of the corner."*

Because our God is unique, we can never place Him in a box. The uniqueness of God should allow our expectations in Him to increase. It should influence our prayer lives and strengthen our faith for the impossible.

God gave us eternal life and power over sin by His uniqueness. Because of Jesus Christ's work on the cross, we can overcome sin and receive salvation through Jesus. Who would send their only son to die for a world that would disown, curse, abuse, and reject Him? This truth makes God unique. John 3:16 says, *"For God so loved the world that he gave his only begotten Son, that whosoever believeth in him should not perish, but have everlasting life.*" This uniqueness of God is the reason for our salvation. It is rooted in love. As God works behind the scenes on your behalf, celebrate His uniqueness. It will and turn your life around, look for something new.

Principle #3

~~~~~~~~~~~
What is sudden to man is not sudden to God.
~~~~~~~~~~~

When God moves in our lives, it is always at the right time. It may appear to be sudden to us, but it is still God's timing. There are no unexpected events or interventions in the eyes of God. God is omniscient. He has all knowledge. He knows every situation you will face in your life. We often think situations in our lives catch our God off guard. When you face dark days in your life, God already knows. Because of our lack of knowledge, many times, God's handiwork may seem sudden. When we understand that God knows all things, this truth should help us to trust Him more.

Genesis 22 is a remarkable story of the sacrifice of Abraham. God knew that the ram would be in the bush before Abraham brought Isaac to be sacrificed. God tells Abraham to take his beloved son Isaac upon the mountainside and to present him as a burnt offering. Abraham is faithful and does what he is told. He takes Isaac to the place

God instructed; builds an altar; lays the wood; and bounds Isaac. Abraham is devoted to God and prepares to sacrifice his son's life as requested.

Genesis 22:13 says, *"And Abraham lifted up his eyes, and looked, and behold behind him a ram caught in a thicket by his horns: and Abraham went and took the ram, and offered him up for a burnt offering instead of his son."* When God witnesses Abraham's obedience as he stretches forth his hand and takes the knife to sacrifice his son, God spares Isaac's life. When we obey God, expect some unexpected blessings. When God works behind the scenes, expect the sudden intervention.

Principle #4

~~~~~~~~~~~

Just because it looks like there is no hope, it doesn't mean God is not near.

~~~~~~~~~~~

It may look hopeless, but the appearance of despair doesn't mean God is not near. God is a God of comeback, turnaround, deliverance, and breaking chains. God is near when you cannot see Him or feel Him. The story of Paul's conversion (Acts 9) is an excellent example of a life nowhere near God, but God was near.

Paul was a persecutor of Christians and the Church. He identifies himself as a chief sinner (1 Timothy 1:15). It appears there is no hope for Paul (the name was Saul). God stepped in and did the miraculous. Just when you think all hope is gone for your unsaved family member, a dead-end job, a struggling marriage, God will perform a miracle. Acts 9:3, 4—*"And as he journeyed, he came near Damascus: and suddenly there shined round about him a light from heaven: And he fell to the earth, and heard a voice saying unto him, Saul, Saul, why persecute thou me?"* Paul had an assignment against the Church, but God intervened in his life, and he was never the same again. You may have loved ones that seem far away from God. You think they will not be saved and have no hope. With a God behind the scenes, they may be closer than you think. One intervention from Jesus can change the whole view. Our God doesn't get tired nor does He stop as we do. I love what the Psalm writer says in chapter 121 verse 4, *"Behold, he that keepeth Israel shall neither slumber nor sleep."*

So the principles, that govern the behind scene moments in our lives are (1) God is moving, even when we don't see it; (2) God is unique; (3) What is sudden to man is not sudden to God; and (4) Just because it looks like there is no hope, it doesn't mean God is not near. God is always behind the scenes on our behalf.

These principles are prevalent in the life of Joseph. Joseph was the favored son of Jacob. God's work in Joseph's life truly shows "behind the scenes" moments (Genesis 37-50). While God is working behind the scenes, Joseph reveals his trust and commitment to God. During multiple seasons of Joseph's life, he was challenged.

God Behind the Scenes _____

Through the life of Joseph, believers can clearly see how God works behind the scenes. Joseph, one of the Old Testament heroes, is a perfect example of trust and surrender to God. Joseph displayed faith through multiple adversities.

SCENE 1

God Behind the Scenes _____

Scene #1
Joseph finds favor.

The favor of God can be described as "tangible evidence" that a person has the approval of the Lord. When we favor someone, we want to be with him. We delight in him. We connect with him in a way that we do not connect with anyone else. We usually favor people who also favor us.

Jacob with Joseph wearing the coat of favor

In his youth, Joseph was known to be favored by his father, Jacob. Why was he so favored? The Bible says, *"because he was the son of his old age."* Jacob favored him so that he showed it outwardly, by making him a coat of many colors (Genesis 37:3). The Bible does not indicate that Joseph flaunted this favor in a negative fashion. This is a powerful point! God favors His children, but it doesn't give us a license to wave it in the face of others. The response to God's favor should be humility. Joseph gave no thought to how his father's favor may have made his brothers feel. Just because we are humbled, with the favor of God, doesn't mean jealousy will not arise in people. Joseph's brother's response to this favor was hatred. Genesis 37:4— *"And when his brethren saw that their father loved him more than all his brethren, they hated him, and could not speak peaceably unto him."* Jealousy can be a silent enemy.

Often, God is blessing other people with so much, and we develop an ungodly feeling toward them. We may not even realize it until it is too late. If you are in this category, I ask you to stop right now and pray. Ask God to change your heart. This sin will grow like a bad disease.

This favor that Joseph receives from his father begins a story that brings trial and tribulation in his life. Yes, we all want favor; but are we willing to pay the cost to have it? We want the blessings of God, but not the things attached to blessings. Job said it this way *"...What? shall we receive good at the hand of God, and shall we not receive evil (2:10)?"* Job is responding to his wife after they lost family and possessions. We must trust the God of "behind the scenes," when we have more than enough or nothing at all. The enemy does not like the favor in your life. Therefore, he will attack you. We must be like Job and understand, *"naked I came into the world and naked I will leave"* (Job 1:21). We may embrace the favor of God, but our love is not in the favor. We see two responses to favor: Joseph and his brothers. Joseph accepts the favor, but he doesn't make it a headline. His brothers see the favor and respond with hatred.

_____God Behind the Scenes

Curtain Challenges from Scene #1

1. How are your responding to the favor in your life?
_____
_____
_____

2. Are you parading God's favor in your life?
_____
_____
_____

3. Are there people you have ill-feelings towards, because of the favor God is showing them?
_____
_____
_____

This page intentionally left blank

SCENE 2

Scene #2
God shows Joseph a dream.

In this scene, there is more separation between Joseph and his brothers. Once a person develops jealousy or hatred for an individual, unless dealt with—the more God blesses him, the greater the hatred increases. Genesis 37:5 says, *"And Joseph dreamed a dream, and he told it his brethren: and they hated him yet the more."*

God gave Joseph the gift of interpreting dreams. It is essential that we see; God is the giver of gifts. As the scenes of Joseph's life unfold, we see that he never took credit for this gift. Joseph's brothers developed more hatred for him. First, he is the favorite son, and now he tells them that he would reign over them (Genesis 37:8). Joseph shared his dream seemly with no evil motives. He was excited about what God showed him. We see that our good intentions may not always be well received.

We must be careful how we share our dreams with others. Some people are "dream killers." The moment they hear your dream, negativity is their response. They will do or say anything to bring doubt to your dream. We may share our dreams with good intentions, but some people are not always ready to hear it. Some people really don't care what God is showing. Dream killers are those individuals who have given up on their dreams or may not have any dreams at all. Be prayerful about the sharing of your dreams. Don't surround yourself with dream killers. They will drain the life out of you in multiple ways.

Joseph's brothers hated him more for his dream, but their hatred did not stop him from dreaming again. He continued to dream (Genesis 37:9). Never allow anyone or anything to stop you from dreaming.

Joseph discusses the dreams with his father and brothers. He tells them that while binding sheaves in the field, their sheaves bowed down to his sheaves. Although Jacob favored Joseph, he was not in agreement with his dream. Jacob's response, *"What is this dream that thou hast dreamed? Shall*

I and thy mother and thy brethren indeed come to bow down ourselves to thee to the earth (Genesis 37:10)?" Remember, even those that love you and are close to you may not embrace the dream God has given you. If God said it to you, He will do everything to bring it to pass. In Scene #1, Joseph finds favor. Scene #2, Joseph has a dream. These two scenes open the curtains for Scene #3.

_____God Behind the Scenes

Curtain Challenges from Scene #2

1. Who are the dream killers in your life?
_____
_____
_____

2. Have you become a dream killer, because it seems things are not moving in your life the way you expected?
_____
_____
_____

3. What is your dream?
_____
_____
_____

This page intentionally left blank

SCENE 3

God Behind the Scenes _____

Scene #3
Satan is always active.

Scene #1 and Scene #2 have Joseph's brothers disgusted with him. The more they saw favor for Joseph; the more hatred stirred in their hearts. Scene #3 introduces Satan's methods to destroy Joseph. Despite how well things are going in your life, the enemy is always devising a plan to destroy you. Peter said in 1 Peter 5:8, *"Be sober, be vigilant; because your adversary the devil, as a roaring lion, walketh about, seeking whom he may devour."* His assignment is to stop the building of God's Kingdom and destroy as many people as possible.

One day, Joseph was instructed to check on his brothers while they were watching their sheep. His brothers plotted against him (Genesis 37:18). Your dream is more significant than Satan's plots. As they are plotting to kill, Rueben heard and said, "let us not kill him (Genesis 37:21)." God is working behind the scene on Joseph's behalf. The brothers' desire to kill him, but God allows Reuben to step in and save him.

Joseph's brother throwing him in the pit.

Rueben's suggestion was to throw Joseph in a pit (Genesis 37:22). When Joseph approached them, they stripped him of his coat and threw him in a pit with no water (Genesis 37:23, 24). They stripped his coat of favor, but the favor or dream were not in the coat. They were connected to God's purpose for Joseph's life. We should never get confused about the blessings and the favor of God in our lives. We love things, but God loves us.

What could be going through the mind of Joseph? One day his father is giving him a coat, he is dreaming dreams, and now he is in an empty pit with no water, left to die. At this moment, many of us would think all is over. The pit is only the holding place for the next position. Don't allow your pit to bring you in despair. Just think, they were talking about killing him, and instead, he is in a pit. While Joseph is sitting in a pit, his brothers are eating bread. Then a company of Ishmeelites came pass, and Judah suggested to sell Joseph to the them.

_____God Behind the Scenes

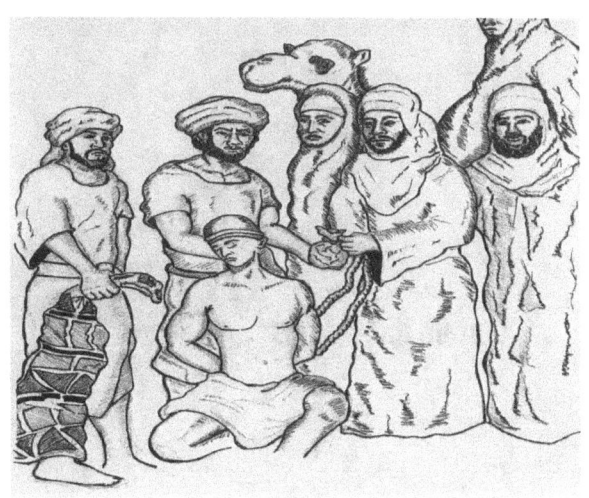

Joseph being sold to the Ishmeelites.

So they pulled Joseph out of the pit and sold him for 20 pieces of silver (Genesis 37:25-28). They brought Joseph to Egypt. Then, the Midianites sold him into Egypt unto Potiphar (Genesis 37:36). Once again, God is working behind the scenes. Joseph was not left in a pit to die. There was no potential with the Midianites.

Therefore, he was sent to Egypt and sold to an officer of Pharaoh. What could Joseph be thinking now? He is in an unfamiliar territory and with unknown people. Scene #3 has shown the attacks of Satan and the attempts to kill Joseph's dream.

God Behind the Scenes _____

Curtain Challenges from Scene #3

1. Has Satan's attacks caused you to doubt your dream?
_____
_____
_____

2. Where can you see God working behind the scene in your pit?
_____
_____
_____

3. Does new places and people cause you fear and doubt?
_____
_____
_____

SCENE 4

Scene #4
The Anointing Recognized

Joseph is now in Potiphar's house (Chapter 39). In the three previous scenes, we see all the attacks against Joseph. He was hated by his brothers because of his father's favor and his dreams, thrown in a pit, and sold twice. At this time, Genesis 37:2 indicates, Joseph was just a young man (17 years old). Such a young age to go through so much. Even though the weight of life came against Joseph, he remained faithful and trusted God. Verses 2 and 3 just blows me away! It says, *"And the Lord was with Joseph, and he was a prosperous man, and he was in the house of his master the Egyptian. And his master saw that the Lord was with him, and that the Lord made all that he did to prosper in his hand."*

As Scene #4 develops, we see God is still with Joseph. Scripture says Joseph was prosperous. Prosperous means successful. Joseph had no control, and God had all control. The Egyptian master saw that the Lord was with him. WOW! What kind of demeanor did this teenager display? An ungodly leader could see God was in him. Joseph obviously had a way about him that he did not look like what he had been through. If we are trusting God to work behind the scenes for us, everyone shouldn't always see our troubles on our faces. Despite what we experience, the anointing still should show. God had not abandoned Joseph. Although Joseph experienced trials and tribulations, God was behind the scenes working out His plan. Joseph has remained faithful to God.

Joseph being traded to Potiphar was a part of the divine plan. Genesis 39:4-6 says, *"And Joseph found grace in his sight, and he served him: and he made him overseer over his house, and all that he had he put into his hand. And it came to pass from the time that he had made him overseer in his house, and over all that he had, that the LORD blessed the Egyptian's house for Joseph's sake; and the blessing of the LORD was upon all that he had in the house, and in the field. And he left all that he had in Joseph's hand; and he knew not ought he had, save the bread which he did eat. And Joseph was a goodly person, and well favoured."*

Joseph, Potiphar, and Potiphar's wife

Joseph has gone from the bottom of the pit to the overseer of Potiphar's house. Potiphar trusted his entire house in the hands of Joseph. God blessed Potiphar's house because Joseph was there. I call this favor overflow. Potiphar's house and field were extremely blessed.

God Behind the Scenes _____

Curtain Challenges from Scene #4

1. Are your troubles affecting your character?
   _____
   _____
   _____

2. Do you look like what you have been through?
   _____
   _____
   _____

3. Can people see your anointing in your anxiety?
   _____
   _____
   _____

SCENE 5

Scene #5
Compromise is Not An Option.

All the attempts to break Joseph did not work, they only deepened the trust in a God behind the scene. When Satan cannot get you to fall in one area of life, he will try another. Jesus says Satan comes only to steal, to kill, and to destroy (John 10:10). Joseph has weathered scenes one through four. Scene #5 presents another challenge to the life of Joseph. After Joseph is all settled in the new position as overseer of Potiphar's house, Potiphar's wife tries seduction (Genesis 39:7).

Potiphar's wife attempts to seduce Joseph.

Don't allow your dreams to die for a few moments of pleasure. Joseph did not let the advances of Potiphar's wife to put him in a place of regret. Joseph refused her advances. He responded both in the natural and the spiritual. He gave respect to Potiphar and his authority, and honored God in one statement. Joseph says, *"There is none greater in this house than I; neither hath he kept back anything from me but thee, because thou art his wife: how then can I do this great wickedness, and sin against God* (Genesis 39:9)?"

Joseph didn't allow himself to get distracted by the voice of the enemy. As believers, we need to acknowledge that the enemy is working behind the scenes in the heart of man and woman. Satan wants to distract us from the dream that God has given. The dreams that God gives us must move beyond material pleasures. If we cannot remove or separate ourselves from the distractions of the enemy, it will be challenging to hold the dreams that have been birthed in our hearts.

Joseph did what he had to do to separate himself. Potiphar's wife was very persistent toward Joseph. She would ask him day by day to lie with her (Genesis 39:10).

So, the final time, Joseph was alone with Potiphar's wife, and she tried to entice him again. She caught him by his garment, and he ran away from her (Genesis 39:12). We cannot entertain temptation, we must flee from it. Joseph could have given into the temptation, but he chose God's will, word, and way. Joseph shows us that there is a way of escape (I Corinthians 10:13).

_____ God Behind the Scenes

Curtain Challenges from Scene #5

1. Does your natural desires supersede your dreams?
_____
_____
_____

2. What temptation have you entertained too long?
_____
_____
_____

3. What distractions are blocking your dream?
_____
_____
_____

This page intentionally left blank

SCENE 6

God Behind the Scenes

**Scene #6
Grace With Potiphar**

In scene #5, Joseph did everything he could to keep himself right before God and Potiphar. One attempt to destroy your character is never enough. Potiphar's wife was not successful in her seduction, so now she lies and accuses him of rape. Of course, Potiphar believed his wife.

Consequently, Potiphar had Joseph thrown into prison. Genesis 39:20 says, *"And Joseph's master took him, and put him into the prison, a place where the king's prisoners were bound: and he was there in prison."* Joseph's refusal or your refusal does not stop the enemy.

Joseph experienced more favor and the grace of God. Potiphar was the captain of the guard, and he dealt graciously with Joseph. He could have just killed Joseph for merely looking at his wife. Not only do we find favor with God, but also with man. Luke 2:52 says, *"And Jesus increased in wisdom and stature, and in favor with God and man."* This is a concept often overlooked or misunderstood. Finding favor with man doesn't mean you compromise your faith or walk with God. It is understanding that God has people in your path that will bless, watch, and support you. We sometimes burn our favor bridges with man.

We see God working behind the scenes (sparing Joseph's life) as he is sent to prison. Although Joseph could not articulate what God was doing in his life, he allowed God to have free reign as He worked behind the scenes.

God Behind the Scenes _____

Curtain Challenges from Scene #6

1. Where have you found favor with man?
_____
_____
_____

2. Where have you seen Satan be persistent in your life?
_____
_____
_____

3. Where has God spared your life?
_____
_____
_____

SCENE 7

Scene #7
Favor in Prison

This favor with man continues in this scene, which is orchestrated by God. Genesis 39:21 says, *"But the LORD was with Joseph, and shewed him mercy, and gave him favor in the sight of the keeper of the prison."*

When we continue to believe God and stay committed to Him, He will continue to open doors in our lives. Joseph continued to work hard and be faithful to God. He was placed in charge of all the prisoners in prison. The captain of the guard charged Joseph with prisoners, and he served them (Genesis 40:4).

Time had passed, and Pharaoh's chief butler and chief baker had offended him. They were placed in the same ward as Joseph. Both the butler and the baker woke one morning after dreaming. They were saddened and unsure what their dreams meant. They told Joseph about the dreams. I love his response. Joseph being in prison, still remain faithful to the giver of his gift. He took no credit. Genesis 40:8 says, *"...And Joseph said unto them, Do not interpretations belong to God? tell me them, I pray you."* They told Joseph about their dreams, in hopes to get the revelation.

Joseph, in prison, interpreting the baker and the butler's dream.

He interpreted and told the chief butler his dream first. Joseph informed the butler that he would be freed and returned to his former position. Joseph interpreted the chief baker's dream. The chief baker would die. Both interpretations proved to be true. The chief baker was hung (Genesis 40:22), and the chief butler was restored (Genesis 40:21). These interpretations were a part of God working behind the scenes to open new doors for Joseph.

_____God Behind the Scenes

Curtain Challenges from Scene #7

1. Has your present situation caused you to stop using your gift?

_____
_____
_____

2. Who has God placed in your life to open doors?

_____
_____
_____

3. Are you being faithful to God through your storm?

_____
_____
_____

This page intentionally left blank

SCENE 8

Scene #8
Your Gift Will Make Room for You

As we come into Scene #8, two years have passed, and Pharaoh has a dream that he did not understand. The Egyptian magicians and wise men could not interpret the dream. The chief butler remembered Joseph's gift and told Pharaoh. Pharaoh summons Joseph. Joseph's initial response to Pharaoh was no different than with the one he gave to the butler and the baker in prison.

When Joseph was brought before Pharaoh, he says, *"...it is not in me: God shall give Pharaoh an answer of peace* (Genesis 41:16)." Joseph interpreted Pharaoh's dream. Joseph could have taken all the credit to get out of prison, but he did succumb to self-gratification. The dream revealed that there will be 7 years of plenty and 7 years of famine. The famine will be so devastating that the years of plenty would not be recognized (Genesis 41:30). After Joseph interprets the dream to Pharaoh and the servants, they were satisfied with the interpretation. Then, Joseph provides wisdom concerning the dream. Genesis 41:34-37 says, *"Let Pharaoh do this, and let him appoint officers over the land, and take up the fifth part of the land of Egypt in the seven plenteous years. And let them gather all the food of those good years that come, and lay up corn under the hand of Pharaoh, and let them keep food in the cities. And that food shall be for store to the land against the seven years of famine, which shall be in the land of Egypt; that the land perish not through the famine. And the thing was right in the eyes of Pharaoh, and in the eyes of all his servants."*

Pharaoh listened to Joseph and was convinced that he had the spirit, wisdom, and discreetness to lead Egypt through the famine. Therefore, Pharaoh positioned Joseph over his house, and no one would be greater than he, accept Pharaoh himself.

God Behind the Scenes

Joseph, the Governor of the land

Pharaoh put his ring on Joseph's hand, gold chain on his neck, and arrayed him in vestures of fine linen (Genesis 41:42). The Egyptians would bow to him. God was working behind the scenes on the heart of Pharaoh. The gift God gave Joseph opened the door for his new season. Proverbs 18:16 says, *"A man's gift maketh room for him, and bringeth him before great men."*

_____God Behind the Scenes

Curtain Challenges from Scene #8

1. Does God get all the credit for your gift?
   _____
   _____
   _____

2. Are you waiting for God to open the doors?
   _____
   _____
   _____

3. Are you parading your gift or is God providing the path for your gift?
   _____
   _____
   _____

This page intentionally left blank

SCENE

9

Scene #9
The Dream Comes to Pass

Joseph is 30 years old. Genesis 41:46 says, "And Joseph was thirty years old when he stood before Pharaoh king of Egypt. And Joseph went out from the presence of Pharaoh, and went throughout all the land of Egypt." Approximately 13 years has passed since Joseph was in slavery. His faithfulness helped him to overcome his challenges and prosper. God working behind the scenes gave Joseph the skills, knowledge, and determination to flourish.

Pharaoh gave him a wife, and she gives birth to two sons. "And Joseph called the name of the firstborn Manasseh: For God, said he, hath made me forget all my toil, and all my father's house. And the name of the second called he Ephraim: For God hath caused me to be fruitful in the land of my affliction (Genesis 41:51-52)."

While Joseph is raising a family, Pharaoh's dream is being manifested, and the famine was in the earth. All countries traveled to Egypt and purchased food from Joseph. Jacob, Joseph's father, tells his sons to go to Egypt to get food.

Joseph's brothers came to Egypt to buy food. Because Joseph was the governor of the land, when his brothers appeared before him, they bowed. When they bowed, Joseph remembered the dream. It is amazing for someone to go through so much that the dream can still be revealed. Seventeen years later, the dream God gave Joseph has now come to past. Joseph tested his brothers and eventually reveals himself to them (Genesis 45:3).

Joseph had every right to take revenge on his brothers, but he gives a kingdom response. Joseph calls them close to him and encourages them not to grieve or be angry for their negative actions towards him. Joseph informs his brothers that it was a part of God's divine plan. God was working behind the scenes to save lives (Genesis 45:5-8). He instructs his brothers to bring their father to Egypt. Then, Joseph kisses his brothers and weeps. The emotions of the family and the

God Behind the Scenes

Joseph embraces his brothers.

 They all came to Egypt and settled in the land Pharaoh gave them. Despite all the evil of his brothers, they are blessed. Genesis 45:16-20, *"And the fame thereof was heard in Pharaoh's house, saying, Joseph's brethren are come: and it pleased Pharaoh well, and his servants. And Pharaoh said unto Joseph, Say unto thy brethren, This do ye; lade your beasts, and go, get you unto the land of Canaan; And take your father and your households, and come unto me: and I will give you the good of the land of Egypt, and ye shall eat the fat of the land. Now thou art commanded, this do ye; take you wagons out of the land of Egypt for your little ones, and for your wives, and bring your father, and come. Also regard not your stuff; for the good of all the land of Egypt is yours."*

God Behind the Scenes _____

Curtain Challenges from Scene #9

1. Are you able to bless those you have mistreated you?

_____
_____
_____

2. Do you allow your emotions to control your responses to people?

_____
_____
_____

3. Can you show genuine love to the person that put your life in danger?

_____
_____
_____

SCENE 10

Scene #10
God Will Turn It Around.

This final scene is based on Genesis 50:20, *"But as for you, ye thought evil against me; but God meant it unto good, to bring to pass, as it is this day, to save much people alive."* Joseph previously alluded to this thought earlier. This scene gives an impactful perspective to all believers. When you know God is working behind the scene, it changes your approach to life, ministry, and people.

After the death of Jacob, his brothers were concerned about their future. They were afraid Joseph would hate and repay them for all the evil. Joseph gave his brothers comforting words. He told them not to fear because he was in the place of God (Genesis 50:19).

Genesis 50:20 identifies the heart of God. We must trust what God allows into our lives. It is for God's greater glory. It only makes sense to put your trust and cares in Him. God is up all night anyway, no need for you and Him to be awake.

Joseph tells them their acts against him were meant for evil, but God meant it for good. Because of Satan's attack, God works behind the scene to work things out for us (Romans 8:28). Everything that took place in Joseph's life, God was there to intervene and orchestrate. We must trust God and be patient throughout the process. In each scene of Joseph's life, God was there. We could always try to remove the scenes from our lives, thinking it will make our lives better.

As said before, if Joseph's brothers never sold him to the Midianites, then Joseph would not have gone to Egypt. If Joseph never went to Egypt, he would not have been sold to Potiphar. If he was never sold to Potiphar, Potiphar's wife never would have falsely accused him of rape. If Potiphar's wife never falsely accused him of rape, then he would not have been sent to prison. If he was never sent to prison, he would not have met Pharaoh's chief baker and chief butler. If Joseph never met the baker and the butler, he never would have interpreted their dreams. If Joseph never interpreted their dreams, Pharaoh would not have known there was someone who could interpret his dream. If Joseph didn't interpret Pharaoh's dream, he wouldn't have become governor of Egypt. If Joseph was never appointed as governor, he would not have been in position to save his family and a nation. What makes this story life changing is because Joseph trusted his God behind the scenes. Joseph lived out Proverbs 3:5, 6—*"Trust in the LORD with all thine heart; and lean not unto thine own understanding. In all thy ways acknowledge him, and he shall direct thy paths."*

_____God Behind the Scenes

Curtain Challenges from Scene #10

1. Have you seen God turn evil in your life for good?

_____
_____
_____

2. Where in your life do you need to trust God more?

_____
_____
_____

3. Are you in the place God wants you to be?

_____
_____
_____

This page intentionally left blank

BEHIND THE SCENES EPILOGUE

Epilogue

I would be remiss, if I did not identify how Joseph's life points to our Risen Savior. God the Father, God the Son, and God the Holy Spirit working behind the scenes to redeem mankind. Let's briefly look at a few of the comparisons.

Betrayed

As we view the life of Joseph and Jesus, we know that God was in control. God knows the heart of every man. He uses their evil works to fulfill His divine plan. Be of good cheer, the evil that is working against you, God has a plan. It may seem as if the assignments are progressing, but Isaiah 54:17 gives the conclusion to every demonic weapon against your life. Simply, "it will not prosper." Both Joseph and Jesus were betrayed by those closest to them. Judas, one of Jesus' disciples betrayed him for 30 pieces of silver (Matthew 26:15). As we just read, Joseph's brothers betrayed him due to jealously. Remember: Satan doesn't fight fair; he will use anyone to destroy your dream.

Put in the Ground

Joseph's brothers threw him in a pit alive. They gave him no water and hoped he would die. On the other hand, Jesus was put in the grave. Although, he had died on the cross first. Hallelujah, on the third day, Jesus rose from the dead! The grave could not hold Jesus down, because a greater plan was already established.

The pit and the grave were temporary placements to bring forth a greater glory to God. Don't allow a temporary place to take your passion. You are coming out!

Suffered Unjustly

Joseph did absolutely nothing to deserve the hatred and the punishment he received. Joseph was tempted in many areas, but he did not lose focus. He was falsely accused, and his character was always put into question. Joseph was the chosen vessel whereby God's plan would be fulfilled. This was the same case for Jesus. Jesus was falsely accused, but He did not say a word (Matthew 27:14). He was made sin for us, so that we may be made righteous (2 Corinthians 5:21). Jesus endured temptation, as we do, yet He did not give in to Satan (Hebrews 4:15). Your suffering is part of the process to bring forth the promise.

Dealt With Starvation

Joseph was given wisdom to overcome seven years of famine in Egypt. With this divine wisdom, many people would have died from starvation, including Joseph's family. At a time when there was no hope, God used Joseph to be the vessel to bring physical deliverance to a nation. Jesus came to satisfy a spiritual starvation, not a physical one. Without Jesus, mankind would still be spiritually-hungry. Matthew 4:4 says, *"But He answered and said, It is written, Man shall not live by bread alone, but by every word that proceedeth out of the mouth of God."* Jesus is our great deliverer. We will always have hope because of His sacrifice.

Set in Powerful Positions

Joseph was elevated to the second highest position in Egypt. God's favor and Joseph's gift of interpretation of dreams opened the door. Pharaoh experienced the anointing of Joseph. Jesus' humility and willingness to do the Father's will placed Him at the right-hand of the Father. He is daily making intercession for us (Romans 8:34). Don't discredit the positions where God places you. He will use you to display His power.

www.ingramcontent.com/pod-product-compliance
Lightning Source LLC
Chambersburg PA
CBHW050444010526
44118CB00013B/1674